To Betsy,
My favorite cousin-in-law!
God bless you and your family always.

Love,
Kathy

THIS WOMAN'S HEART

Kathleen Berck-Parker

WESTBOW
PRESS
A DIVISION OF THOMAS NELSON
& ZONDERVAN

Copyright © 2014 Kathleen Berck-Parker.

All rights reserved. No part of this book may be used or reproduced by any means, graphic, electronic, or mechanical, including photocopying, recording, taping or by any information storage retrieval system without the written permission of the publisher except in the case of brief quotations embodied in critical articles and reviews.

WestBow Press books may be ordered through booksellers or by contacting:

WestBow Press
A Division of Thomas Nelson & Zondervan
1663 Liberty Drive
Bloomington, IN 47403
www.westbowpress.com
1 (866) 928-1240

Because of the dynamic nature of the Internet, any web addresses or links contained in this book may have changed since publication and may no longer be valid. The views expressed in this work are solely those of the author and do not necessarily reflect the views of the publisher, and the publisher hereby disclaims any responsibility for them.

Any people depicted in stock imagery provided by Thinkstock are models, and such images are being used for illustrative purposes only. Certain stock imagery © Thinkstock.

ISBN: 978-1-4908-5157-0 (sc)
ISBN: 978-1-4908-5158-7 (e)

Library of Congress Control Number: 2014916152

Printed in the United States of America.

WestBow Press rev. date: 09/09/14

CONTENTS

A WOMAN'S HEART - GOD'S DWELLING PLACE..........1
TO LIVE IS CHRIST 3
HE KNOWS MY NAME 4
JESUS HEALS 5
I AM HERE 6
FOREVER FAITHFUL 7
FLY AWAY 8
GLIMPSES 10
GROWING 12
PHIL 4 13
FREE INDEED 14
GOD WILL 16
GOD'S STILL HERE 18
IT'S ME LORD 19
JOY AND SORROW 20
LASTING BEAUTY 21
LOSS AND GAIN 22
LOVE ANYWAY 24
MUSIC OF MY HEART 25
NOT FORGOTTEN 26
ONCE AGAIN 27
ONE DAY 28
PEACE, BE STILL 29
PRAISE #1 31
PRAISE #2 32
PRAISE #3 33

REMIND ME	34
RUN TO HIM	35
SO CLOSE	36
SO REAL	37
STANDING	39
TEARDROPS	40
PURPOSE	41
YOU ALONE	42
THE CHURCH	43
WAITING	45
THIS LIFE	46
YOU CHOSE ME	47
UNCLOUDED VISION	49
BRAND NEW	50
TIME THAT IS TO COME	51
THE TRUTH	52
THANK YOU	53
LIFE CYCLES	54
I WILL SEE HIM	55
A PRAYER OF THANKS IN THE PARK	56
ABIDE IN HIM	57
ABOVE THE CLOUDS	58
ANSWERS	59
BECOMING	60
CHARACTER, NOT COMFORT	61
EVENING PRAYER	62
FAITH	63
LOVE LETTER	64
SEASONS	65
A BRAND NEW YEAR	67
BLESS YOU MOTHER	69

GRANDMA'S MOTHER'S DAY POEM	70
MOTHER'S LOVE	71
POEM FOR MOTHER'S DAY	73
FATHER'S DAY	75
PATRIOTIC SUNDAY	76
SEPTEMBER 11, 2001	77
CHRISTMAS MEMORIES	78
FAMILY CHRISTMAS	79
THE GIFT	81
SPRING SACRIFICE	82
EASTER REFLECTION	83
RESURRECTION MORNING	84
THANKSGIVING	86
AFTER THE FIRES	87
GOOD-BYE FRIEND	88
HAPPY BIRTHDAY FRIEND	89
GOLDEN FRIENDS	90
MY FRIEND GLEN	92
MY FRIEND LOU	93
VISITING A FRIEND	94
THREE VALENTINES	95
POEM FOR AMY	97
AMY'S KITTY	98
CATY'S HAIR	99
NATEY'S POEM	100
SHANNAN THE BRAVE	101
MY NIECES	103
DAUGHTER-IN-LOVE	105
FOR CHRIS	106
MY DAUGHTER, MY HEART	108
SIXTIETH BIRTHDAY	110

LOVE'S HEARTACHE 112
LOVE'S TRAP 113
DO YOU REMEMBER ME? 114
A NEW NAME 115
ALL ABOUT YOU 116
IN MY HEART 117

DEDICATION 119
END NOTES 121

A WOMAN'S HEART - GOD'S DWELLING PLACE

A woman's heart, God's dwelling place,
where peace and love reside
and Father, Son and Spirit are welcomed to abide.

Within that heart is found a space for family and friends
and a quiet place where she has stored
sweet memories to tend.

Deep within those chambers her children's sounds are scattered,
along with precious images
of those times that really mattered.

Marriage, birth and even death are pictures that she keeps,
of smiles collected through the years
and tears when grief was deep.

The conversations and the prayers of
friends that she holds dear;
the many fun times that she had
are all abiding here.

This house has hidden nooks to store a
woman's dreams and sorrows
and shelves to keep her joys and fears
and hopes for her tomorrows.

But the largest and the best of rooms is for the honored guest -
where only God may dwell within
to comfort, save and bless.

This holy place is where she meets her Maker and her friend,
where God reveals the hidden things
and where love never ends.

TO LIVE IS CHRIST

To live is Christ, to die is gain
This life you live is not in vain
Each thing you do with God in mind
Each thought you have, each mountain climbed
Will bring you closer to His throne
Each step you take will lead toward home
To Him whose arms are open wide
Christ longs to have you by His side
When face to face you'll clearly see
and live with Him eternally
Though you may strive and give your all
You'll sometimes stumble, sometimes fall
Yet, Christ is with you all the way
And He will listen when you pray
He'll see each tear and hear each cry
He'll answer when you ask Him why?
Just keep on reaching for the prize
That He has set before your eyes
Do not give up or bow to pain
For to live is Christ to die is gain

HE KNOWS MY NAME

He formed my frame, He knows my name
In His bottle are my tears
My days He planned by His mighty hand
He carries all my fears

I cannot hide for He's by my side
no matter where I roam
He shines His light in the darkest night
and leads me to my home

There is no fear with my Savior near
my worries are in vain
He erased my sin when He took me in
and forgot my guilt and shame

He is my joy, He is my peace
He leads me as a lamb
Toward His glorious light, where there is no night
to Christ the great I Am

JESUS HEALS

(Written in church while listening to a sermon
about "The Sermon On the Mount")

There was not one He turned away
among the crowds upon that day
they came with bruised and broken lives
and pain reflected in their eyes
He knew about their dreams and goals
He saw the sickness in their souls
but as they came He knew each one
deep in their hearts and what they'd done
He saved their souls and gave new life
and freed them from their years of strife
He healed them all of their disease
then brought the healed ones to their knees
for when they met him face to face
and felt His love, compassion, grace;
their hearts of stone were rearranged
and lives forevermore were changed

I AM HERE

(Paraphrase - Exley)

Beloved child, please do not fear tomorrow
And do not dread the things that you can't see
Your ignorance does not hold cause for sorrow
Since what you do not know, is known to Me

I see the past, the present and the future
I know what lies before you in this life
I see the obstacles that block your journey
And the reasons why you go through pain and strife

It's easy to rejoice when you are happy
And your life is going well and you're content
But it's harder to be thankful to the Father
When all is darkness and your soul is spent

If you would only realize your problems
Are given to you just to make you strong
And though you cannot understand the reasons
I will turn your deepest cries into a song

Please remember I am with you every moment
I feel your pain and also see your tears
With each step I'm here, I'm walking right beside you
So my precious child, surrender all your fears

FOREVER FAITHFUL

The Lord is faithful, forever faithful
He'll always be right by our side
He knows about our many failures
Yet his arms are opened wide

His love is boundless, knows no measure
It is not possible to hide
Our sinful thoughts and careless actions
Our envy or our stubborn pride

We are not faithful, as He's faithful
We let the world distract us so
Our time is spent on selfish things
We're always busy, on the go

We come to him when times are bad
and seldom thank Him for the good
We don't take time to talk to Him
or read his Word the way we should

But still He's faithful, forever faithful
He will not leave us on our own
The work He started He will finish
Until the day He calls us home

FLY AWAY
(Psalm 55:6-8)

From time to time when life gets rough
and it seems my best isn't good enough
I long for something so much more
and respite from my daily chores

On the wings of a dove
I would fly away
To a place of safety and rest from today
On a mountaintop by a lake of blue
I would take a nap and dream of You

I would not spend time on questions there
or contemplate the why or where
but would be content just to sit awhile
thinking lovely thoughts that would make me smile

A gentle breeze would caress my face
And a soft perfume would surround the place
The song of birds as they fly above
would remind me of God's care and love

Peace and contentment fill my mind
as I leave the cares and stress behind
God whispers softly in my ear
Be still my child, I am always here

Then as all good things must have an end
I would smile and start my day again
Giving thanks to God for my getaway
Yet…. how I would love to fly away!

GLIMPSES

This day began and seemed to be just like so many others
My desire was to stay in bed and snuggle 'neath the covers
But something pulled me from my
bed and drew me to the door
So I opened it, not knowing what the day might have in store

The sun was just behind the hills, it had not fully risen
And I realized the special gift that God to me had given
Displayed in perfect splendor for my sleepy eyes to see
was a glimpse of heaven's glory and a hint of what's to be

A sunrise that was beautiful and glorious to behold
was revealed to me in colors of yellow, red and gold
I caught my breath and stared in awe at this most brilliant light
I bowed my head and thanked the
Lord for giving me this sight

Most days I am so busy that I seldom take the time
To look around and see the beauty in this life of mine
My loved ones and the special friends that God has given me
The wonder of each tiny flower, the mountains and the seas

For the infinite variety of all God has created
Leaves a hunger and a thirst in me for a better life awaited
Each glimpse is just a foretaste of eternal life to be
And I cherish every moment I am loved, and blessed and free

So until I take my final breath, I'll have to wait awhile
And for now I have to be content to appreciate and smile
At hints and little glimpses of what God has planned for me
When I arrive at my forever home to dwell eternally

GROWING

Every heartbeat, every tear, every sorrow while we're here
Every suffering, every pain, everything we failed to gain
Was sent by God to make us grow, to
help us see, to let us know
that one day it will all make sense, when we see the evidence
of Christ and what He did for us, that
He is loving, wise and just
For when we die and leave this place
and we see Jesus face to face
We then will know as we are known, and with all joy shout
"I am home!"

PHIL 4

Whatever's right, whatever's pure,
Whatever's lovely, true and sure
My heart will dwell upon such things
Then peace will come and my soul sing

God always meets my every need
Before I ask my prayers He heeds
He's always there each time I call
He will provide - my all in all

He gives me strength for all I do
I know He loves me through and through
Throughout my life and every day
He is the life, the truth, the way

FREE INDEED

I knew that you were watching Lord when I was all alone
and wondering if I'd ever find a love to call my own
then I pledged myself to a special man
and I fell in love to stay
I believed our love was real and true
when I gave my heart that day
I meant the vows I made to him when I promised to be true
Forever was the dream I had and my
world seemed bright and new
I really felt our love would last until the end of time
Whatever I had would be his and his would all be mine
but although in the beginning, our love was sweet and pure
as years went by, his feelings changed
and he said he was unsure
He doubted that he'd ever loved the person that I was
though I had changed, he stayed the
same, our differences the cause
so we parted ways and I spent my days
feeling lonely and afraid
Dwelling in the past and thinking back to mistakes I'd made
In a daze I cried and ached inside as
I dealt with all the wrongs
I cried out to you and asked what to do
and for strength to carry on
Now ten years have passed, I can say at
last, new peace and joy I've gained

I've learned to forgive and let God
heal the sorrow and the pain
He has dried my tears through the lonely
years and fulfilled my every need
Christ is by my side and I'm satisfied, for I am free indeed

GOD WILL

Psalm 73:26

"My flesh and my heart may fail, but God is the strength of my heart and my portion forever."

When my heart is hurting
When my body is aching
When my hopes are fading
God strengthens me

When I feel let down
When my joy's not found
When my smile is gone
God lifts me

When I cannot rest
When my mind's a mess
When my peace has left
God comforts me

So I'll give my best
In each daily test
I must not give up
God loves me

Yes, God loves me so
He will not let go
He will be my guide
and walk by my side

Every single day
As I go my way
Blessing me with grace
Till I see His face
God saves me

GOD'S STILL HERE

God's still here, He has not gone away,
God's still here, and He is here to stay
In your darkest hour, in your deepest fears
God's still here.

When you are lost, feeling full of doubt
when you are wondering what life is all about
Call His name, He will hear your cry
and He will tell you why
God's still here.

Do not give up, you are not alone
Do not let go, kneel before the throne
Just tell Him all, He has seen your tears
and all your lonely years
God's still here.

Lift your burdens up and He will carry you
Ask for peace, He will see you through
When your faith is weak, when your hope is gone
You can carry on - God's still here.

IT'S ME LORD

It's me Lord, asking You to love me
It's me Lord, asking You to free me
It's me Lord, asking You to hear me
It's me Lord, asking You to heal me

I don't need to ask Lord -
You have already loved me, freed me
heard me and healed me
You have also saved me, blessed me,
used me and sealed me

I am at peace Lord
I am still
I am abiding
In Your will

JOY AND SORROW

Lord, I admit I do not understand
why joy and sorrow both come from Your hand
It seems that daily troubles multiply
Yet, every day You open up my eyes
to give me glimpses of the little things
that You have blessed me with…and my soul sings!

My weeping may be there throughout the night
But mercies wait for me with morning light
and even though this trial's a mystery
I know I'm Yours throughout eternity
I'll take Your hand in mine and will not fear
Because I know, my Jesus you are near.

LASTING BEAUTY

The world looks on the outside
and ignores what lies within
too many judge a woman's worth
on whether she is thin
ignoring things like character,
integrity and trust
the world looks on the outward shape
and what inspires lust
but when a woman loves the Lord
her beauty bubbles forth
and her standing in the eyes of God
is the measure of her worth
In quietness and purity
she goes about her days
loving God and helping others
who she meets along the way
when she looks into a mirror
and beholds her form and face
she sees a lovely bride of Christ
and a sinner saved by grace
in God's eyes she is perfect
and He lets her know she's loved
don't set you sights on things of earth
but your bridegroom up above

LOSS AND GAIN

I've suffered loss throughout my life
Had disappointments, pain and strife
Some friends who once beside me stood
Are gone and left without a word

Dear family members passed away
those memories will never fade
A marriage once good, fell apart
and left a whole inside my heart

My children grew and left our home
And don't have the time to telephone
With work and interests in their lives
but of course, I'm happy that they thrive

I'm facing old age on my own
and have regrets for things undone
Alone and without love to share
with a special person waiting there

But every loss has been a gain
I've learned to smile, embrace the pain
Without the loneliness and tears
Without the sadness and the fears

I would not be the person who
depends on You the way I do
I do not know the when or how
But I will be content for now

LOVE ANYWAY

How do we love with hearts full of pain?
How do we give when there's nothing to gain?
How do we serve when our strength is all gone?
How do we hope when we've waited so long?

When we serve and we try, yet our efforts are poor
When we don't get our way and we always want more
When we swallow our pride and our best dreams all die
When we struggle in vain, hang our heads and just cry

Well - we love anyway which lessens our pain
We give anyway and a blessing we gain
We rely on God's strength and we pray on and on
And we just keep on waiting, cling to Him and hold on

God will do as He says, all His words are so true
He will dry every tear and be waiting for you
He will fill you with strength and your hopes will fulfill
Just ask Him to help you - He can and He will!

MUSIC OF MY HEART
(Ephesians 5:19)

You are the music of my heart
the song I sing in the deepest part
When all is dark and my soul seems lost
I sing about the matchless cost

The beauty you have made on earth
the price you paid to give me worth
Are reasons for the praise I sing
My soul takes flight on grateful wings

My spirit plays the melody
of what in love you gave for me
The harmony is like a prayer
from me to show You that I care

My praise wells up and overflows
with joy and peace to Him who knows
this love song is for only Him
Then my soul is at rest again

NOT FORGOTTEN

Sweet music played alone, a lonely sound
the notes of sorrow floating all around
a once full life, now empty, incomplete
searching for some peace and pains' release
An isolated time of inner growth
reflections of my mind and those missed most
arriving at a place where hope resides
a deep deep yearning fills my soul inside
My heart leaps up to grasp the slender straw
of hope held forth and I am in God's awe
that once again He's here to comfort me
reminding me of joy that's meant to be
I'm not forgotten, for I am His child
I once knew love, I laughed and cared and smiled
I know that I will be myself again
I'll cast aside my sadness and I'll win
For truly God is here and loves me still
I yield to Him my heart, my soul, my will

(This was written just before my marriage of 23 years ended. Praise God, I am happy and content today in 2014).

ONCE AGAIN

It's been a year since you've been gone
And I'm still here, my life goes on
I know you're in a better place
But oh! I long to see your face
The pain and sadness I still feel
The loneliness is very real
I've had some good times and some bad
But the memories of what we had
Give comfort, and they make me smile
For I know that in a little while
We'll be together once again
And our love and joy will have no end
God promises eternal life
Where there's no crying, pain or strife
So to this promise I will cling
Beneath the shelter of His wings

ONE DAY

Every heartbreak, every tear
every sorrow while we're here
every suffering, every pain
everything we failed to gain
has been sent to make us grow
to help us see, to let us know
that one day it will all make sense
when we see the evidence
of Christ and what He's done for us
that He is loving, wise and just
for when we die and leave this place
and we see Jesus face to face
we then will know as we are known
and with all joy shout "I am home"!

PEACE, BE STILL

There is nothing that's too hard for You
and this was something that I knew
so many times Your love had proved
hearts can change and mountains move

Believing in Your power and grace
and seeking You upon my face,
I knew for sure that what I ask
would be for You an easy task

The deceiver whispered not to plan
on help or answers from God's hand
discouragement, depression, fear
was all he wanted me to hear

So my doubts refused to leave
my thoughts were dark and unrelieved
as Satan with his lying ways
tormented me both night and day

But just when I was in despair
with thoughts of failure everywhere
my mind in turmoil, full of doubt
and wondering how it would turn out

Before I prayed to You again
about my need and heart of pain,
You had already answered me
in ways I could not hope to see

The Father's voice spoke truth to me
and gave me hope so tenderly
Because my prayers were in His will
the great I AM said, "Peace, be still."

Sorrow came to me at night
but joy was in the morning light
I saw that nothing would escape
the love and power of His embrace

Christ is my hope, my joy, my friend
My time with Him will have no end
These present troubles all will cease
and I will find eternal peace

PRAISE #1

I will not wonder how you came
to set the stars in place
I will not wonder how the moon
and sun were set in space
I will not question how you know
the numbers of each hair
I will not wonder why you love
or why you're always there
I will not ask the question why
You've blessed me with your grace
or why you saved me from my sins
and covered me with grace
I'll only praise you for your works
which are wondrous things to see
I'll only praise you for your love
and that you've chosen me

PRAISE #2

Praise for living one more day
Praise for a place my head to lay
Praise for food you daily send
Praise for grace that has no end
Praise for friends and family
Praise for love you give to me
Praise for strength to carry on
Praise for peace and victories won
Praise for causing me to sing
Praise you God for everything

My hope and strength in you alone
Will be my only cry
And sheltered here beneath your wings
I'll remain until I die
Then leaving all my cares behind
my earthly life will pass
and I'll fall upon my knees
and say "Praise God! I'm home at last!"

PRAISE #3

As I lay upon my comfy bed
I thank you for the day ahead
Thank you for my house and car
Thank you for my life so far
I praise you for providing me
With everything so generously
Praise you that You're always near
and when I call You, that You hear
I know You're watching up above
I praise you Jesus for Your love

REMIND ME

Down in the depths of despair and depression
I cried out my pain to the Lord
Help me dear Savior to feel your compassion
Help me remember Your words

Remind me oh Jesus of my many blessings
Remind me of Your precious love
Lift up my spirit out of the darkness
Send me some strength from above

Then Jesus the Comforter spoke to my spirit
And with me He came to abide
He whispered "I love you" and said "I won't leave you"
"I will always be right by your side"

Then joy and gratitude filled all my being
And I felt such a welcomed release
As Jesus, my Savior, Redeemer and Friend
Restored to me joy and great peace

RUN TO HIM

Amazing peace, joy and love
showered down from God above
Washing us in waves of grace
As we lift our hands in praise

Power, faith and hope are mine
Glimpses of new life divine
The Holy Spirit teaching true
of the One who died for me and you

Praise the Father, Praise the Son
For who They are and what They've done
Praise the Spirit for the way
He intercedes and helps us pray

Our eyes will one day see His face
We'll understand His love and grace
He'll call our name, we'll run to Him
Then our new lives will begin

SO CLOSE
(Psalm 34:18)

The Lord is close to the brokenhearted
He sees our tears and hears our sighs
When days are dark and full of worry
He lifts our souls and dries our eyes

He saves those who are crushed in spirit
by giving hope; providing peace
The Lord redeems His faithful servants
From pain and suffering brings relief

Taste and see the Lord's great goodness
Flowing down from up above
Know the joy of His forgiveness
Feel the power of His great love

He has promised to be near us
and to keep us by His side
We never have to be alone
For in our hearts He will abide

SO REAL

Jesus is so real to me
God's one and only son
I wish that He would come to me
and share my earthly home

I can picture Him just sitting here
On a chair right at my table
As I tell Him of the day I've had
and of all that I am able

If only for a little while
we would sing and laugh and talk
I would tell Him of my troubles
as together we would walk

He would listen closely as I speak
With loving eyes so kind
He would nod His head or laugh aloud
and wouldn't seem to mind

As I tell him all about my dreams
and share with Him my fears
He would understand my pain and doubts
and would dry away my tears

I would feel love and compassion
unconditional and free
And see His scars and realize
the price He paid for me

He would leave a glow inside my heart
I would want Him so to stay
But the peace I'd feel inside my soul
Would not quickly fade away

"I'm always here each time you call
I'm so happy you believe"
"I will return", He would say to me
and prepare to take His leave

Then enfolding me within His arms
He would hold me to His heart
And whisper words of peace and hope
And then quietly depart

STANDING

There are days I feel unworthy, disgusted and ashamed
sometimes I feel so guilty and myself accuse and blame
Even though I know His promises to me are sure and true
There are moments when I stumble
and I don't know what to do

I know who is accusing me, I know who's telling lies
it is Satan whispering doubts to me and then I realize
I do not need to listen when he tells me I am lost
I only need to cling to Christ who's already paid the cost

I have to stand upon God's Word and the enemy will flee
He has no right to harm my soul and no authority
My hope is built on Christ alone and no one can replace
the love I know He has for me, no evil can erase

For when I wallow in the depths of darkness and despair
My God says "Peace, I love you child - I am always here.
You cannot quench my love for you,
for I chose you from the start
and nothing that you do or say can change the smallest part
of all the joy you've given Me, you're the apple of My eye
some day when you are home with Me,
you'll know the reasons why"

TEARDROPS

There is a bottle filled with tears
that I have shed throughout the years
For God has saved each teardrop cried
and with each one I'm sanctified
He sees my fears and all my sorrows
He knows each hope for my tomorrows
One day the bottle will be full
Then off to Jesus I will go
where my tears will be no more
when I reach that peaceful shore

PURPOSE

Our purpose is to love our God
with heart and soul and mind
to love our neighbors as ourselves,
and show them how to find
The joy and peace salvation brings
transcending space and time
and how to help those people who
are hopeless, scared and blind

Our purpose is to teach the lost
about the truth we know
To help them as they seek to learn
and encourage them to grow
And when they've learned to trust the Lord
and their faith is strong and true
To join them as they worship God
in all they say and do

Equipping them to do the things
that God has called them to
and standing there right by their side
until their journey's through

YOU ALONE
(Psalm 86)

You alone are God
there is none but You
and I will ever praise You
For the wondrous things You do

You alone are God
Before the world began
You planned to set eternity
into the hearts of men

You alone are God
and by Your grace I'm saved
Your love is great and I'm delivered
from a dark cold grave

You alone are God
Your love for me is true
and I will spend my lifetime
In faith and praise to You

THE CHURCH

Every member on a mission
Each one glad to do their part
With the Holy Spirit's guidance
and a passion in their hearts

Going forth to tell the story
of Christ's love and sacrifice
and the Good News of His mercy
changing hearts and giving life

Showing by their faithful service
that they love as Christ has loved
with thankfulness for all the gifts
from their Father up above

Standing tall upon the shoulders
of the ones who went before
who showed by their example
freedom is worth fighting for

And the task that God has given
is to share with every man
His word, in which He has revealed
His truth and His great plan

So until Christ comes to get His Church
we still have much work to do
For the Church will never cease to be
until our work is through

WAITING

Here I am Lord stilled and waiting
quiet and anticipating
hoping to begin anew
and wondering what I should do
You have a goal, a plan for me
You always have, but I can't see
what it might be or where to go
and how to get there, I don't know
My heart's desire is to serve
but I'm afraid, I haven't nerve
to try the things I do not know
and find a different way to grow
I'm full of doubt and imperfection
praying for Your wise direction
seeking strength and power too
for the good works I must do
I know You love me, I won't fear
You'll walk with me, I know You're near
You'll give me peace and hold my hand
and with that knowledge I can stand
My hope and trust in You alone
will be my guide and lead me home
I'll hear your voice, Your face I'll see
"Well done my servant - come to Me"

THIS LIFE

With all life's cares and worries
ever pressing on our minds
It's hard to laugh or feel the joy that God wants us to find
When troubles come into our lives
it's so easy to give in
To pity and discouragement which opens doors to sin
It's not His plan for us to be
defeated or depressed
He wants us to enjoy each day and give our hearts a rest
Abundant life and joy are ours
to embrace and call our own
Just remember God has promised we will never be alone.

YOU CHOSE ME
(Love Song - Isaiah 53:6)

We all like sheep have gone astray
and each of us has turned to our own way
What was it Lord that made You love me so?
I may not ever know
why You chose me

You searched my heart to see if I
would follow You and not deny,
the price You paid to set me free
by sacrifice upon the tree
and You chose me

You saw my frame before I came
into this world and no one knew my name
You planned each day beginning to the end
and I wonder once again
why You chose me

Of all the people in this world that You could choose
You knew that I would never lose
the love for You that burned inside
that I would never try to hide
but always serve You faithfully
and You chose me

My life will never be the same
for You have given me a name,
a hope, a peace, and family
Yes, I am oh so thankful
You chose me

UNCLOUDED VISION

Sometimes my vision is unclear
obscured by worry, doubt and fear
and all I see throughout the day
are people and problems in my way

Flowers are reaching for the sun
stars are shining when night has come
but my mind is focused on the things
that living in this world can bring

When I take the time to really see
the many blessings surrounding me
and forget about my daily cares
I am so thankful and aware

Of the beauty in each brand new day
and when I take the time to pray
my heart fills up with joy and pleasure
for God has given me this treasure

To see this life through Heaven's eyes
makes me lift my head and realize
that each day's a gift to open up
grace is overflowing from my cup

BRAND NEW

The Lord is making all things new
His promises are always true
He shapes and molds us as He will
to form us into something real
He helps us understand the lies
that cloud our vision and our lives

The pieces of our broken hearts
the shameful deeds which were a part
of life before we knew the Lord
He shapes into a scarlet cord
that Satan cannot break or use
to demoralize or to accuse

Then Jesus in His loving ways
invades our thoughts and lights our days
What once was old and scarred inside
is now renewed and glorified

We need not dwell upon the past
For He has set us free at last
His love is changing all we do
For God is making all things new

TIME THAT IS TO COME

**Between the poles of love and almost hate
lies joy, suspended from a slender thread
Some lovers find the secret out too late
long after passion dies and love has fled**

Moving forward in small slow steps
hour by hour and minute by minute
as days go by when there are no steps at all
and time stands still
but, there is mostly forward motion now

Emerging out of dense fog in a blur of emotions
laced with uncertainty, pain and fear
A fine balancing act between love and hate
finally evolving into acceptance
as if there is a choice

Coming to terms with the past
and making peace with the future without fear
Bittersweet melancholy memories remain in my heart
they are all that remain today

Hope arrives unexpectedly in prophetic dreams
and morning brings with it a sweet surprise
The peaceful feeling of forgiveness at last
a prayer of thanks for the chance to begin again
and maybe this time get it right

THE TRUTH

When I am old and weak, do not turn your back on me or leave me alone. I have an enemy who wants me to die alone and without hope. He is a liar who tells me I am worthless. Non-believers tell me that my God has left me and there is no one to save me. But God, be near to me and save me quickly. Show all my accusers that you are real and put them to shame. Cover them with scorn and disgrace. Prove them wrong! (Psalm 71:9-13 paraphrased).

Pilate asked Jesus "What is truth"? Jesus answered - "I came into this world to testify to the truth". When our enemy, Satan, opens his mouth only lies spew forth. He is the father of lies and yet we oftentimes believe him when he tells us we are worthless, ignorant, ugly, helpless and weak. Why are we so quick to believe him when we know where to find the truth? Jesus tells us what the truth is in his Word. We don't have to believe the lies. Jesus says we are worthy. We are so valuable that he died for us. We don't have to be ignorant - we only have to ask for His wisdom. We are not helpless. The God of Angel Armies is always by our side and fights our battles for us. We don't have to feel ugly. God looks on the heart and not on the outward appearance. He sees us as His beautiful and most special creation. We don't have to feel weak. We can do all things through Christ who gives us strength. So, the next time Satan is whispering his lies, remember who you are in Christ and rejoice. You are special and loved and completely forgiven.

THANK YOU

Thank you for your grace Lord
and the strength for each new day
Thank you for the people Lord
who I meet throughout each day

Thank you for your faithfulness
for your mercy and your love
Thank you for the home that's mine
in your Heaven up above

Thank you for forgiving me
of each and every sin
Thank you for the promise
that together we will win!

LIFE CYCLES

A life begins, another ends
and so the cycle starts again
the joy and sorrow taking place
both sad and happy; pain and grace

The infant's cry, the senior's sigh
one first hello, one last good-bye
a family's peace, a loved one's grief
the spark of life, an ember ceased

New life with possibilities
a life well-lived, then given ease
one sent from Heaven full of worth
one back to Heaven from this earth

The fresh new body growing steady
the tired body old and ready
exciting things to learn and do
a long hard journey now is through

Life cycles are what all must face
as young or old we run the race
But when our time on earth is through
Jesus welcomes us with life anew

I WILL SEE HIM

My eyes will see His holy face
I'll understand His love and grace
He'll call my name and hold me close
then I will know I'm finally home

How glorious that I will hear
the songs of angels sweet and clear
Singing praises to His majesty
and I will know why He saved me

When He rewards me with my crowns
I will kneel and cast them down
where they belong at Jesus' feet
and then my joy will be complete

For as I walk the golden streets
beside the crystal river sweet
and see the tree of life divine
I'll know I'm His and He is mine

I'll feel no more the hurt and pain
and never cry or grieve again
For all He promised He will do
My soul eternal, clean and new

A PRAYER OF THANKS IN THE PARK

Thank you for this quiet moment Lord. Thank you for this pretty park and the green grass and the trees. Thank you for the sound of children playing on the playground and of family picnics and the joy of watching families playing together. Thank you for the shade this big old tree is providing and for the breeze that refreshes me.

Lord, please help that person who is collecting cans for money. I am thankful for all you have given to me. Help me not to take things for granted but to always realize that everything I have and everything I need comes from you. Help me to know that I am just one paycheck or one phone call away from losing everything and that could be me collecting cans. It is only by your grace that I am alive and well and not in need.

Most of all Lord, thank you for the answer to prayer this week. Thank you for being faithful to me when my faith in you was weak. Thank you for using the time of waiting on you to help me grow. Thank you for being more interested in my character than my comfort.

I love you Lord, you know my heart. Help me to rely on you for everything because I know that my next heartbeat and my next breath are gifts from you. Continue to mold me into the person you saved me to be. Reveal your will to me and show me the path I should take. Use me to further your kingdom.

AMEN

ABIDE IN HIM

Abide in Him when your way seems dark and lonely
Abide in Him when you feel that you're the only
one who knows the pain and hurt that you are feeling
and your mind and body need some spiritual healing
Abide in Him.

Abide in Him when your worry and your fears have overtaken
Abide in Him as your faith and hope are weak and being shaken
and your heart and soul are tired, bruised and worn
and you question why and say you can't go on
Abide in Him

Abide in Him for He's always there to listen
Abide in Him and He'll provide what you are missing
He'll replace your deepest fears with joy and peace
He will comfort you and bring you sweet release
Abide in Him

He will dry your tears and give you hope to see
what your life will be with Him eternally
He'll show you that this world's not all there is
That your life is precious and new life He'll give
To those who place their faith and trust in Him

      So the answer is to just - Abide in Him

ABOVE THE CLOUDS

Looking out the window at a sea of clouds below
as far as the horizon spans, I see the sun's bright glow
now and then the vista clears and the earth is emerald green
dotted here and there with trees, and
diamond lakes or streams
suddenly the landscape shows small
buildings, roads and homes
is this the way it seems to God as He
watches from His throne?
I know as He looks down on man while to and fro we dart
He sees us individually and knows what's in each heart
each one He sees is special, each person's soul His prize
and everyone who calls on Him is precious in His eyes
we must appear likes specks to Him,
yet He can name each one
and He loves us with an awesome love,
so much He sent His Son
as I fly back to my home on earth in
this plane that's made by man
I can rest in the assurance that He holds me in His hands
for I know that someday I will fly to
my other home with Him
when my joy and peace will be complete
and my new life will begin

ANSWERS

In the ebb and flow it's hard to know
what each new day will bring
The mysteries and joys of life are often puzzling things
We wake up every morning with anticipation high
Then the day goes on and we begin to question reasons why

Depression over news we read and helplessness we feel
all reaffirm suspicions that our worries are quite real
What can we do to change the world?
What difference can we make?
How is our life supposed to count
when the news is full of hate?

The answer doesn't lie in what the world might say is true
and it doesn't stem from anything that we may say or do
So we must look to a higher place
where truth and love abound
Where peace and grace are evident
for our answers to be found

We must place our trust in God alone who is always in control
we know His plans are for our good and to help us learn and grow
Yes, we must admit that we don't know
and we haven't got a clue
But we trust the One who is all wise for
His wisdom to shine through.

BECOMING

My soul is longing for a place
full of quiet joy and beauty
where the sense of time and space
knows no care or pressured duty.

My heart longs to hear the singing
of some music soft and clear
as the soul its burden flinging
casts aside each doubt and fear.

Where is that place my mind envisions,
where the air is pure and clean
and the rain is gently falling
on the meadows sweet and green?

Is it only in my distant future
when my being leaves this night
that all the hopes I dream and nurture
Will break forth and come to light?

Or can a soul not yet perfected
catch a glimpse of heavenly places
and by that glimpse be resurrected
to a form that God embraces?

CHARACTER, NOT COMFORT

It's hard to grow when all is going well
when life is great and all our fortunes swell
It's hard to know the peace that Jesus gives
when we have everything we need to live

If times are good and go as we have planned
how do we sense the blessings from His hand?
He sends the times of trouble for our growth
It's our character He wants and values most

He does not use the strongest or the wise
but broken vessels are His biggest prize
The failures of our lives He'll mold until
we become devoted subjects to His will

We learn through our adversity to see
Christ makes us into what we need to be
Our comfort is of little consequence
compared to the rewards that He will send
Be strong when God is disciplining you
For He's only doing what is best for you

EVENING PRAYER

Lord, as I lay down on my bed
I pray that you will give
A safe and happy home to those
I love, in which to live

And may your peace descend on them,
protect and keep them warm
Surround them with your angels
to guard them from all harm

Then when they wake to each new day
may they feel your presence near
to comfort and to guide them
free from every doubt and fear

FAITH

Even though I cannot see what the future has in store
and the world tells me that miracles don't happen anymore
Even though I did not talk with Jesus
when He walked this earth
and the world will criticize me and say I have no worth

I have faith that what is hidden is as real as what I see
that God designed my life before I even learned to breathe
I don't have to hear Him speaking or look into His face
to know that I have been set free and forgiven by His grace

Faith makes all hard things possible, keeps hope alive within
God says "yes" when all say "no" and
His truth says I will win
Faith casts all doubts and fears aside,
opens blinded eyes to see
that what God says He'll surely do
when I trust His plans for me

LOVE LETTER

God who would I be without Your love for me?
How would I know which way to go?
I never want to live in a world devoid of You -
I only want to be aware that You are always there
Beside me as I finish out this life

Then, when I finally look into Your eyes
And You call me by my name
I will realize the life I knew is over and I gain
The promise of eternal life that You made possible for me
And any crowns that You may give, I give back gratefully.

As I walk the streets of gold and worship at Your feet
In the light of all Your holiness my joy will be complete
My tears all dry, my burdens gone, my
pain and suffering ceased
Throughout eternity with You in perfect love and peace.

SEASONS

Staying outside with our friends until the setting sun
warmth of days upon the beach, the barbecues and fun
picnics at the park and lake, and swimming in the pool
vacations to the mountains and the time away from school
are coming to a close so soon we hardly saw them go
the time will soon be here at last to play in winter snow
as summer slowly fades away to be replaced with fall
cooler days and colder nights are welcomed here by all
now leaves of yellow, gold and red are floating softly down
covering every inch below as they blanket the hard ground
pumpkins, ghosts and witches decorate the homes and yards
and fireplaces months unused send smoke into the clouds
the grass once lush and emerald green
is sparse and turning brown
and the air is clean and crisply cold as
it whistles through the town
shouts are heard all over as some folks cheer football winners
and families gather happily to enjoy their turkey dinners
calls from loved ones are received with laughter or with tears
and thanks are humbly given for the blessings had this year
then snowflakes fall and all the world
is white and crystal clean
with holly wreaths and Christmas
trees, the smell of evergreens
the joy on children's faces as they make their Christmas lists
and the stress on parent's faces as they strive to fill each wish

The songs of many choirs fill the air with sweetest chords
churches packed with worshippers
give praise to Christ the Lord
But soon the cold and frigid air gives way to warmer days
and winter fades into the spring with flowers on display
the winter chill is over and our lives are born anew
the earth blooms into colors of yellow, pink and blue
on Easter morn we give our thanks
that the Lord has truly risen
because He lives believers have the gift of life He's given
And now we've come full circle for another year has past
looking forward to this summer, just as we did the last
the seasons come and then they go as we travel on our way
giving thanks to God above for the beauty of each day

A BRAND NEW YEAR

A brand new year, what will it be?
a time for opportunities
a time to listen to our hearts
to try new things, to have fresh starts,
to pause, reflect and make a change
to toss what's old and rearrange
or do just what we've done before
and wish that we had done much more

This year might be the one we choose
to take that trip, go on a cruise
or maybe stop the grind and rest
to give the family our best
spend time with precious aging folks
to hear their stories and their jokes
they have much wisdom to impart
and love to share from giving hearts

Let's take a day and watch a child,
who may be calm or a little wild
but in those tiny eyes we'll see,
some glimpses of eternity
their innocence and trusting ways
can show us how to live our days
and find the joy in simple things
that every day will surely bring

Yes, very soon this year will be
a portion of the legacy
we leave to those who come behind us,
so let your days be filled with kindness
please don't look back, but look ahead
forget what's past, let go instead
each day's a gift from God above,
to be thankful for and show our love

BLESS YOU MOTHER

I ask the Lord to bless you mother
I wouldn't want to have another
Sweet memories of how you kissed
Each boo-boo when I failed or missed
The times when you stayed up all night
When I was sick or had a fright
The way you made me feel so great
Even when I made mistakes

I remember when I was a kid
and all the crazy things I did
You never tried to make me be
anyone instead of me
You recognized my special gifts
and with kind words gave me a lift
You always taught me wrong from right
and prayed for me both day and night

I listened as you read God's Word
You may not think so, but I heard
The lessons that you gave to me
will stay with me eternally
With all my heart may God above
Bless you mom, the one I love
More beautiful than all the rest
I hope you know, you are the best!

GRANDMA'S MOTHER'S DAY POEM

Ill always luv u
I love you to the moon and back,
I love you here and there,
I love you everywhere.
I will love you everywhere!

2014 Mother's Day poem
Caitlyn P. Your granddaughter (9 yrs. old)

(In its original form, this poem was in an extremely large font and each letter was a different color. Caty spent a great deal of time on it).

MOTHER'S LOVE

I have a feeling deep inside
and it is like no other
it's warm and gentle, strong and true
it's the love I have for mother

It matters not what place I'm in,
of if we're near or far apart
Mom holds a spot reserved for her
living deep within my heart

It's in a place where no one else -
not child, dad, sister; brother
can enter into at their will
that spot belongs to mother

A cozy place where I can go
when life's too much for me
and where I gain the strength
to become what I should be

Sometimes I go into that place
and shed some bitter tears
sometimes I go in just to think
of memories through the years

And there are times I go to laugh
or talk to her awhile
sometimes I just go there to sit
and think about her smile

And each time that I visit her
I'm like a child again
I know she loves me for myself
on that I can depend

Each one of us preserves this place
deep in our souls to hide
for nothing but our mother's love
makes us feel so good inside

POEM FOR MOTHER'S DAY

Mom, I owe you everything
You taught me all I know
You helped me learn to walk and talk
and fed me so I'd grow

You kissed all of my scratches
when I was hurt at play
and dried my tears when I was sad
You brightened up my day

When I was scared you held me close
and made it seem all right
When I was sick you cared for me
and stayed up through the night

You liked to play fun games with me
and taught me right from wrong
You knew just where to tickle me
and you sang my favorite songs

You taught me how to love the Lord
and showed me how to share
with kids who didn't have as much
or had no one to care

So Happy Mother's Day to you
I hope your day is fun
'Cause of all the moms in this whole world
You are the greatest one!

FATHER'S DAY

When I was just a little girl and would crawl up on your lap
You would tell me I was pretty and we'd talk of this and that
And you told me very often to be all that I could be
How to never be afraid to try and to live with honesty

The lessons that you taught me I've remembered through the years
and I often think about them and they always bring me cheer
I have so many memories of our good times in the past
Of vacations and the games we played, we really had a blast!

Dad you've always been there for me, you've never let me down
I know that I am in your heart even though you're not around
I will always be that little girl who you snuggled on your shoulder
My love for you will never change, though we're both a little older

So Happy Father's Day to you - Dad you deserve the best
I would never ask for someone else, you are greater than the rest
You have molded me and shaped me into what I've grown to be
Thanks for all the sacrifices and the love you've shown to me.

PATRIOTIC SUNDAY

(Written in church July, 1997)

Our God has made it so
a nation strong and free
this country that began
by faith and liberty
found by fathers who believed
that in order to survive
it must be built on a faith
in the One who gives us life
if we turn our backs on Him
and forsake the faith we knew
then our nation will be gone
and our future will be through
we must cling to what is right
and not let our thoughts be swayed
we must hold on to the truth
nor forget to hope and pray
we are called to be the ones
who seek God to guide our way
with the Light that leads us on
through the strife and towards the dawn

SEPTEMBER 11, 2001

Where was God, some people ask, on that September day?
Did he turn his back on suffering, did he look the other way?
As evil had its way with us, as many screamed and died.
Were the ears of God closed to their cries?
Were His eyes not opened wide?

Our innocence was shattered, our safety, peace and pride.
The glass and smoke were everywhere -
there was no place to hide.
Though no one has the answer for how these things could be.
The truth is God has love so great, He allows us to be free.

He grants each soul the gift to choose the path that it will take
The freedom to do good and bad, to shine or make mistakes.
But this one thing is absolute and all we need to know -
Despite the terror and the pain, our God is in control.

CHRISTMAS MEMORIES

All holidays are special, but Christmas seems the best.
There's a certain kind of glow you feel
that's missing from the rest
The Christmas trees so fragrant, the mistletoe and lights,
the decorations and the gifts, the candles glowing bright
Fond memories of Christmas past grow
sweeter through the years
Remembrance of our families, with laughter, joy and tears
And with each year the holiness of this most blessed night
returns to us and fills our souls with
hope that's burning bright
So our hearts are full at Christmastime
with love for one another
and thankfulness to God above for His gift above all others
The sacred gift we have received is the Babe born in a stall
For God sent us His only Son to come and save us all

FAMILY CHRISTMAS

The memories of long ago surround us on this night
The music softly playing, the candles and the lights
The warmth and happy feelings with all our loved ones near
is something that we cherish at this special time of year
We love to get together with our friends and family
To sing the carols, share the food and laugh so merrily
To see the faces of the kids as they close their eyes and wish
And the joy on parents' faces as they see them get their gifts

Yet on this night we realize that there are those we miss
Our relatives who've gone before - we long to hug and kiss
For they're the ones who always made our holidays so great
Who bought our gifts, set up the tree and helped to decorate
They gave us bikes, and toys and dolls
and spent the extra time
Just to buy one special present when they didn't have a dime
They drove us out to look at lights
while we were safe and warm
Then stayed up late on Christmas Eve
and rose early Christmas morn

And even though they're gone now, we feel they are a part
Of our gathering this Christmas and
we hold them in our hearts
We remember them and miss the love
we shared while they were here

As we hold them close inside our hearts,
we smile and feel them near
They would not want us to be sad, but would want us to enjoy
This night which celebrates the birth of the blessed baby boy
For the sacrifices that they made, for their love year after year
We remember them and strive to carry on what they held dear
We hope that they are looking down
and enjoying what they see
For time and space can never change the bond of family.

THE GIFT

It is not about the presents
the tinsel or the lights
But about the Son of God
born to us that night

What a blessing to rejoice with friends
and celebrate the season
Yet throughout the busy days and nights
We forget He is the reason

The birth of Jesus was the gift
from God to mortal man
To bridge the gap that sin had made
when He reached out His hand

No gift we give to others can
compare to what was given
When our Father opened wide His arms
and showered us from Heaven.

SPRING SACRIFICE

Christ died for us upon that tree, His life's blood flowing down
With hands and feet nailed to the tree
On His head, a thorny crown

Suspended there, His heart laid bare while enduring grief and pain
His sacrifice provided life
With eternity our gain

His love was shown, each sin was known, as He suffered agony
Forsaken there, our sins to bear
God did not intercede

"Father forgive and do not blame, for they know not what they do"
"It's finished" was His final cry
as the debt He paid was through

There was no way that we could pay the price owed for our sin
So with pain and strife, He gave His life
Then He rose to live again

Because the stone was rolled away, our hope is now secure
And death no longer has its sting
For our heavenly home is sure

EASTER REFLECTION

I'm sorry that You died upon that tree
I'm sorry for the blood You shed for me
I'm sorry for Your brow so torn and bruised
I'm sorry for Your body so abused

The price You paid for me on that dark day
Is a debt that I have no way to repay
My gratitude is all I have to give
With surrender to the One who makes me live

My sin had separated God from me
but You died to give me life eternally
The tomb was empty for You had become
the first of those whose victory is won

For when You rose from death that Easter morn
It meant for me a chance to be reborn
And sin no longer has a hold on me
Because You set me free on Calvary

RESURRECTION MORNING

The women were defeated as they made their way that day
down the path and to the tomb where the precious Savior lay
their steps were slow and heavy, their
faces drawn and strained
they felt the loss so deeply of all that they had gained
for when the Lord had come to them,
He freed their souls to sing
they felt their lives had joy and worth
that only He could bring
sleep had been impossible all through the endless night
the images of pain and blood, the horror and the fright
of seeing one they loved so dearly scourged and crucified
they felt as if all hope in them had also bled and died
so carrying the spices and the cloths to wrap Him in
their bodies full of sorrow and with tears that vision dimmed
they made their way down to the tomb
with the stone so heavy there
and as they neared the garden tomb,
an earthquake shook the air
the stone was moved and rolled away
from the entrance they could see
as the women shook with fear and awe
and fell upon their knees
they made their way down to the cave
and looked into the gloom

but all they saw were cast off clothes
and the empty barren tomb
a brightness like no other shown and an angel sat inside
He told them not to be afraid, "Where
is the Lord, they cried?"
"He is not here; and He has risen, just as He said He would.
Come and see where He was lain, then go and tell the world."
So as the women ran away to share what they'd been seeing
The Lord himself appeared to them
speaking softly to them "Greetings".
They came to Him and bowing down
they worshiped at His feet
For when He arose, His triumph over
death was now complete.

THANKSGIVING

I am thankful to be living in a place that's safe and free
with assurance that no one will try to take my liberty
I'm so thankful for my family both near and far away
and for the dear departed ones, who I'll see again one day
For the blessings that are showered on me by the Lord above
and the knowledge that He saved me and that I'm greatly loved
I am thankful that I have a home and have enough to eat
for health and strength to live each day and that my life is sweet
I am thankful for the gifts I have and can use to serve the Lord
and for sharing things with some others what they cannot afford
I'm blessed beyond what I deserve and I know it to be true
that the only reason that I'm breathing is because of You
So thank you once again dear Lord, I give you all my praise
for walking with me through this world as I live out my days

AFTER THE FIRES
2003

The smoke has all subsided and the raging fires contained
and those who lost so many things begin to breathe again.
From the ruins of their broken dreams the spark of hope ignites
and dimly through the smoke and haze they see a distant light.

Though an evil one intended to snuff out joy and peace,
God sent some people who were good; kind folks who gave relief;
these people sacrificed their time for ones they did not know,
and went without their comfort and helped when asked to go

The things that really mattered when all was said and done
were not accumulations lost but the battles that were won
For those who lost their loved ones to the aftermath of pain
For those whose homes were rubble and will have to start again

We say do not lose courage; don't give in to grief and pain
shed your tears and dry them quickly then begin your lives again
Although it's hard to start from scratch your lives are on the verge
and from the ashes of your dreams new beginnings will emerge

GOOD-BYE FRIEND

It's hard to say good-bye to you
you've been my dearest friend
but just because you're leaving
doesn't mean our friendship ends
'cause it doesn't matter where you are
or if we're near or far apart
I hope you know that even so
you have a place inside my heart

HAPPY BIRTHDAY FRIEND

People who always give of themselves without
expecting anything in return, deserve to have
only good things come their way.
So because you are one of those special people, I am wishing
for you, all of the dreams you have wished for to come true.
Because if anyone deserves happiness it is you.
Happy Birthday my friend. From someone whose
life you have touched in a special way.

GOLDEN FRIENDS

**"Make new friends but keep the old
One is silver and the other's gold"**........

New friends are made of silver
Old friends are made of gold
They both are very precious
and their worth cannot be told

Some friends are just "hello" friends
Whom you meet throughout the day
Some friends are just the ones you see
When you want to laugh or play

But old friends know your secrets
and they know your deepest needs
They know your past and present
and will pray down on their knees

Old friends are all the ones who know
When you need to pray and cry
They're the ones you call at any hour
and they'll never ask you why

And when you have some news to tell
about how God has blessed you
They're the first to holler "Praise the Lord"
to rejoice and laugh right with you

So, even though you say good-bye
and move many miles away
The bond we have as friends remains
and in our prayers you'll stay

Yes, even though we say good-bye
It will only be awhile
Until we see your face again
And we'll hug and laugh and smile

Forever friends we'll always be
Whether near or far apart
"Soul Sisters" to the very end
and connected with our hearts

MY FRIEND GLEN

I have a friend named Glen
who I visit now and then
We love to talk and laugh
and share stories of the past

Sometimes he falls from bed
and gets cuts upon his head
but he always has a smile
and dresses with great style

He likes Pepsi-Cola best
and he likes to get his rest
but each time I come to call
He gets up and has a ball

Glen is ninety-six years old
and is proud when he is told
that in 4 more years he'll be
an entire century

I'm a very lucky gal
to say that Glen's my pal
He's a very special man
I'm so proud to call him friend

(SADLY, MY FRIEND GLEN PASSED AWAY WITHIN A WEEK OF ME READING THIS POEM TO HIM. I WILL NOT FORGET HIM).
6-2014

MY FRIEND LOU

One day I prayed the Lord would send
someone to be my friend
I asked Him for somebody who
would know and understand
Someone to laugh and cry with,
to talk to and to hear
about the struggles that I have
with those I hold most dear
Someone to serve and dream with,
someone to share my fears
someone to sing and pray with,
someone to dry my tears
So the Lord did as I asked Him
because He sent me you
and now I don't just have a friend
but a "sister" who's named Lou.

VISITING A FRIEND

Majestic mountains topped with snow
deep valleys lush and green below
a river flowing swift and deep
the stillness just before I sleep
Display of stars and moon glow light
Warm conversations late at night
The song of birds and fluttering wings
A distant train's low whistling
The prayers and laughter oh so sweet
These are the memories I'll keep
The bonds of friendship growing stronger
The wish to stay a little longer
The promise made to come again
I do not want this time to end
So thank you for this time together
The azure skies, the pleasant weather
your hospitality was great
I'm coming back - I cannot wait!

THREE VALENTINES

#1
You're so special, you're so neat
and when I kiss you, you're so sweet
So why not make my life complete?
and throw yourself upon my feet!

Please say yes for I love you so
My heart will break if you say no
I can't go on without you near
Oh! Happy Valentines my dear!

#2
There's a place inside my lonely heart
that's waiting just for you
Will you come and fill it up? If not, I'll be so blue
I think about you every night and long for you each day
My love is sure, my love is true; I will not ever stray

There may be others who have said
they will love you, but pretend
to love you as they say they will, but my love will have no end
So pay no heed to what they say, for our love is meant to be
I love you dear with all my heart, please give your love to me

#3

I have not told you how I feel,
it's so hard for me to show it.
When I'm with you my knees get weak
when I try to speak I blow it!
So I am sending you this note to tell
what I'm too shy to express.
I love you more than words can say
Oh, I'm just a lovesick mess!
I can only hope that you might feel
the same way that I do.
Happy Valentine's my love
My heart belongs to you.

POEM FOR AMY

Freckles and a turned up nose
chubby legs and rounded tummy
sometimes silly, sometimes sad
always cute and always funny

Full of questions all the time
and full of love for mom and daddy
Amy you're a special girl
but you're driving us a little batty!

AMY'S KITTY

Amy sat beside the door, beside the door she sat
She looked around and up and down but could not find her cat
Oh, why must he be missing thought poor Amy with a sigh.
I miss him when he's not around. I think I'm going to cry!
So if he doesn't come home soon I think that I will look
in kitty's favorite napping place down by the rippling brook
He loves to go and lie there and stretch out in the sun.
I like to stretch out right beside to talk and have some fun.
We usually play until the sun has started to go down
and then I gather up my things to walk back into town.
But, if my precious furry friend does not come home tonight
I'll have to leave some milk for him
and turn on the porch light
Did I just hear a soft meow from somewhere in that tree?
Oh, goodness, it's my kitty and he's crying out for me
He climbed so high up in the tree and he's so scared and sad
I had better call a fire truck or get my mom and dad
I won't be happy till I'm holding kitty close to me
'cause when we're both together, we're as happy as can be

CATY'S HAIR

I know a cute girl named Caty Potaty
Sweet as can be with a brother named Natey
She has curly hair and when she arises
Her hair is quite messy and full of surprises

Why, Grandma would not be surprised there to see
a nest full of birdies - at least two or three
She might find a squirrel or something that's fluffy
Hard to say what you'll find in hair that's so puffy

The only way Grandma can make it look nice
is to give her a bath and wet her hair twice
Then she sprays and brushes each tangle that's there
until Caty emerges with smooth, shiny hair

She looks very pretty with her head full of curls
and everyone comments "What a beautiful girl"!
But nobody knows what a problem it's been
for poor Grandma to make it as neat as a pin

NATEY'S POEM

Natey is a happy boy, he's funny and he's sweet
He likes to play with Hot Wheels and
ride up and down the street
Videos and DVD's are what he likes to see
and he likes to play with all his friends and visit family
And when he goes to grandma's house they have a lot of fun
They read great books, make cookies and swim out in the sun
Sometimes they go to movies, sometimes stay in and play
They go to church or to the mall and there's always lots to say
When grandma says it's time for bed
Natey takes a bath and brushes
He says his prayers, they sing some
songs and he very rarely fusses
His grandmas and his grandpas, his mommy and his dad
His baby sister and his aunts and uncles all are glad
That they have Natey in their lives to help him grow and love
Each day they are so thankful for this gift from God above

SHANNAN THE BRAVE

There once was a girl named Shannan the Brave
who lived with her parents in the back of a cave
Shannan was tall and quite thin for her size
with lovely brown hair and enormous blue eyes
she lived in a cave instead of a house
because the pet Shannan loved most was a mouse
the mouse was an orphan she wanted to keep
but its manners were awful and it often would squeak
the mouse was so cute still her mother refused
so they packed all their things and to the cave moved
mom said even though not allowed in her home
they would live in a cave so the mousy could roam
One day when Shannan was lying around
from somewhere below she heard a strange sound
she could see something moving but she just didn't know
if the thing would be friendly or if it would go
Shannan was not alarmed or even afraid
she had to be smart, there were plans to be made
she remembered her angel who was always around
and she knew she'd be safe with whatever she found
so she quietly climbed down the hill she was on
and as she walked down she sang her best song
"You Are My Sunshine" she sang as she went
it was her favorite which she learned from her Aunt
when she was in trouble or just missing her dad
she would sing her best song and forget to be sad

as she walked down the hill Shannan gave a quick wave
to her mommy who stood in the front of the cave
"Where are you going?" Shannan's mom asked her daughter
she answered "Downhill, just to get us some water."
When she got to the bottom and looked all about
she found trouble brewing and gave a great shout
for what she discovered in the brush by the cave
was a family of mice that she needed to save
a cat had them cornered with some under his paws
there was one in his mouth and a few in his claws
so now it was time for dear Shannan the Brave
to summon her courage and make the big save
first she chased off the cat by shouting "scat scat!"
gently laying the mice in her pretty straw hat
the mean cat tried to claw her but she didn't worry
she just put on some speed and ran back in a hurry
then she took them inside to their mommy, the mouse
Shannan's mom was so proud they moved back to their house
You can look the world over and you'll never find
a girl who's so smart, so sweet and so kind
She'll come to your rescue and be there to save
For there's no one who's braver than Shannan the Brave

MY NIECES
(Shannan, Payten, & Emily)

They were once so sweet and small
sometimes it's hard now to recall
when they were just my baby nieces
I always loved them all to pieces

Endless books to them I read
had pillow fights upon their beds
each colored page and special craft
held on the fridge with magnets fast

Taking walks and playing games
calling each one silly names
like "Kiki", "Nay-Nay", "P-Nut; "Ham"
Oh, what a lot of fun we had

Their favorite dinners that I cooked
The funny photos that we took
The way they looked while sound asleep
are special memories that I keep

But when I wasn't paying heed
I turned around and they were teens
and time had caused them all to grow
into young ladies all aglow

They still are sweet, but not so small
they go to school and to the mall
their time is spent on phones and boys
and make-up, hair and grown-up toys

It makes me proud to see them grow
they love their auntie, this I know
in my life they play a special part
each one is loved and has my heart

DAUGHTER-IN-LOVE

The daughter who's been mine from birth
cannot be matched for she was first
She's always filled my life with pride
My love for her can't be denied

But there's another daughter who
my son was smart enough to choose
She's made my son a happy home
and with her love he's changed and grown

The grandkids that to me she's given
have been a gift sent straight from Heaven
I wouldn't trade her for another
I've grown to love her like a mother

I hope these words somehow convey
The joy that she brings every day
So blessed she's in our family
Yes, she has my heart eternally.

FOR CHRIS

My firstborn child, my wanted son, I prayed for you to love
I asked the Lord to bless my life with this present from above
I waited so impatiently for your birth day to arrive
Then I heard your first cry and I knew
I'd been waiting all my life

The moment that I looked into your beautiful blue eyes
I instantly became your mom and I could not help but cry
I felt I never would allow anyone to cause you pain
I would protect and comfort you and my hopes were not in vain

Your soft blond hair, your perfect shape, your eyes and little toes
Were wonders bringing me such joy as each new day arose
I couldn't way to show you off to friends and family
I was sure no mom had ever loved her child as much as me

I watched you thrive and grow each day as you began to walk
and I will not forget the time that you first laughed and talked
You went to school, played in sports
and joined the marching band
I watched with pride as you became a kind and loving man

But I blinked my eyes and you were off to a college far away
It was time for you to go, although I wanted you to stay
You visited from time to time and we always had great fun
spending time just reminiscing about the things we'd done

Then you met a woman who would be the one you'd waited for
and my heart was full because I knew you had someone to adore
She filled up all the places that were missing in your life
and when you asked, she answered yes
and said she'd be your wife

So you married and began your life with Gina by your side
You had a son and daughter which filled my heart with pride
Making me a grandma gave me so much happiness
I did not know that I could be so privileged and blessed

Nathan was your firstborn child so you know the way I felt
when I held you in my arms and you made my heart just melt
When Caty came along I knew you marveled just like me
when I gave birth to your sister and increased our family

You're an awesome dad and husband and a special son to me
as the years have passed my mind is
full of precious memories
I am so blessed to be your mom and I thank the Lord above
For that December years ago when He gave me you to love

MY DAUGHTER, MY HEART

Young women dream about the time
when they might be a mother
And think about the blessings of the
birth of their own daughter
They think about her growing up and what her life might be
Of graduation, marriage and the start of family

And I was just like all the rest who thought about these things
I dreamed about how she would look
and what her life would bring
As she grew up would she believe in Jesus up above?
Would she be wild or sweet and kind,
would she return my love?

I wondered if she'd sing with me as I did with my mother
I hoped that she would be my friend
and not want to have another
I worried sometimes as she grew that we might fuss and fight
Or if I'd have to wait for her when she stayed out at night

My hope for her was that she be a person people liked
I wished that she would always strive
to do that which was right
I wanted to instill in her compassion for the lost
And a willingness to stand for Christ, no matter what the cost

My prayers for her were that she have a full and happy life
Free from the worries of this world
with its sadness and its strife
God answered all my hopes and prayers,
for Amy's kind and smart
So beautiful inside and out - she will always have my heart

SIXTIETH BIRTHDAY

Sixty years of life is really quite a lot of living
So many years of learning, so many years of giving
I wondered when I was a child just what my life would be
If I would be a mother and have a family

I dreamed so often in my youth and hoped to reach the stars
But day by day my life evolved and I suffered loss and scars
So I settled for a different life and let my best dreams die
I found myself a little lost and often asking why

But thinking back across the years and milestones I've achieved
The family and friends I have and all that I believe
With wisdom that has come with age and truths I've realized
I know the mountains that I climbed
were just lessons in disguise

Yes if I've learned just one true thing about my life on earth
It's that God made everyone unique
and each life has great worth
Even when I'm feeling lonely, sad, discouraged or annoyed
Every day that God has given me is His gift to be enjoyed

The way to look back on my life is to know how far I've come
and be thankful for the good and bad and all I've seen and done
To let go of all the hurts and pain, to forgive, but don't forget
That even though I'm sixty - my life's not over yet

The best years of my life can be the last years that I'm here
God still has some work for me and I do not need to fear
He has been beside me through this life and will be eternally
So I anxiously await to see what else He's planned for me.

LOVE'S HEARTACHE

Love has many changing faces
as it goes through all its phases
It astounds, delights, amazes
all who enter into love

Everything seems so much brighter
the heart is glad, the steps much lighter
with promise for a happy life
no time to think of pain or strife

But love can also be a heartache
and its weight become a burden
when the bloom has finally faded
and your joy has turned to hurting

Disappointment comes to those
who place their hopes on love alone
and never stop to speculate
that love has gone and it's too late

LOVE'S TRAP

Love is blind I've always heard;
It's also deaf and dumb.
It makes you feel alive and free,
but it also makes you numb!

Love wraps itself around your heart
and makes your spirits dance.
It creeps into your soul and mind
and you haven't got a chance!

So if you fall into love's trap
don't try to get away,
for it will catch you soon enough
and you'll be forced to stay!

DO YOU REMEMBER ME?

Do you remember love
when we were young and free?
Can you recall our joy?
Do you remember me?

Beneath gray skies of fall,
our silhouettes were one.
The beating of our hearts
was our September song.

December came and went,
with spring not far behind.
Our passions all were spent
on dreams too hard to find.

And when the summer came,
we knew it couldn't last.
We said our sad good-byes
Love slipped into the past

Now many years have gone
my first love's a memory
but I wonder now and then,
Do you remember me?

A NEW NAME
(Psalm 147:4 Psalm 139 and Revelation 2:17)

God knows the number of each star
and calls them all my name
He knows the evil in my heart but loves me just the same
Each hair is numbered on my head,
He knows my every thought
Yet He forgives and with His life, my salvation He has bought
When all is dark, He is the light which guides me on the way
He'll never leave me on my own, but walks with me each day
Before I think or do a thing, He knows what I will do
Each day is known to Him alone until my life is through
And some day He will give to me a new name on a stone
And greet me with His open arms and
say "Child, welcome home".

ALL ABOUT YOU

This always has been and always will be
It's all about You and not about me
Sometimes I forget my place on this road
And I selfishly think I can handle the load
I try hard to shoulder the burden alone
And I struggle to carry it all on my own
Without even asking for help to succeed
I mumble and groan and with others I plead
While the One who is able to meet every need
Is just waiting for me to give up and concede
That I need him and I cannot do it alone
Then gives strength and assurance that I am His own
So the next time I'll try to remember to see
That it's all about Jesus and not about me

IN MY HEART

If you look into my heart, this is what you'll find
My Jesus living there, in this heart of mine
I invited him to come, so many years ago
And that is where He's stayed, He loves me this I know
Yet, there have been some days, I could not feel Him near
My heart felt cold and empty, and filled with doubts and fear
But when I read His word, and prayed to feel his might
He warmed my heart of stone with His mercy and His light
God never lets me go, even when my faith is weak
He promises I'll find Him when I call to Him and seek.

DEDICATION

To my parents, Betty and Duane Berck, who always believed in me and encouraged me to express myself. I'll see you at Heaven's gate.

For my children, Amy and Chris; my daughter-in-love, Gina; and my grandchildren, Nathan and Caitlyn; who inspired some of these poems and who give me so much joy.

To my sissy, Karen; my little brother, Tim and their children. I am so happy to be your sister and aunt.

Many thanks to Gwen Ash of Westbow Press who answered each one of my many e-mails with patience and grace and guided me throughout this whole process.

Most importantly, to my Lord and Savior, Jesus, who gave me the ability to write and the reasons to praise. Without Him I would be nothing.

END NOTES

Dear Reader: The poems in this book have been collecting dust in an old brief case, some of them for 50 years. I encourage you to dust off your dreams, use your God-given talent, whatever it may be, and cross that dream off your bucket list, just as I did. But most of all, I encourage you to get to know the God of the Universe through his Word and to have a personal relationship with his son, Jesus. If my poems help you in any way to do that, I am truly humble. Every word of every poem, comes straight from this woman's heart and I pray that they bless you.

The author would love to hear from you at KParker63@verizon.net

CPSIA information can be obtained at www.ICGtesting.com
Printed in the USA
BVOW04s1954031114

373490BV00001BA/2/P